Günter Gerngross • Herbert Puchta

PLAYWAY 1

ACTIVITY BOOK

HELBLING

Hello

1 

1 Look and speak. Colour Linda, Benny and Max.

2

❷ Listen and tick (CD 1/1).

3 

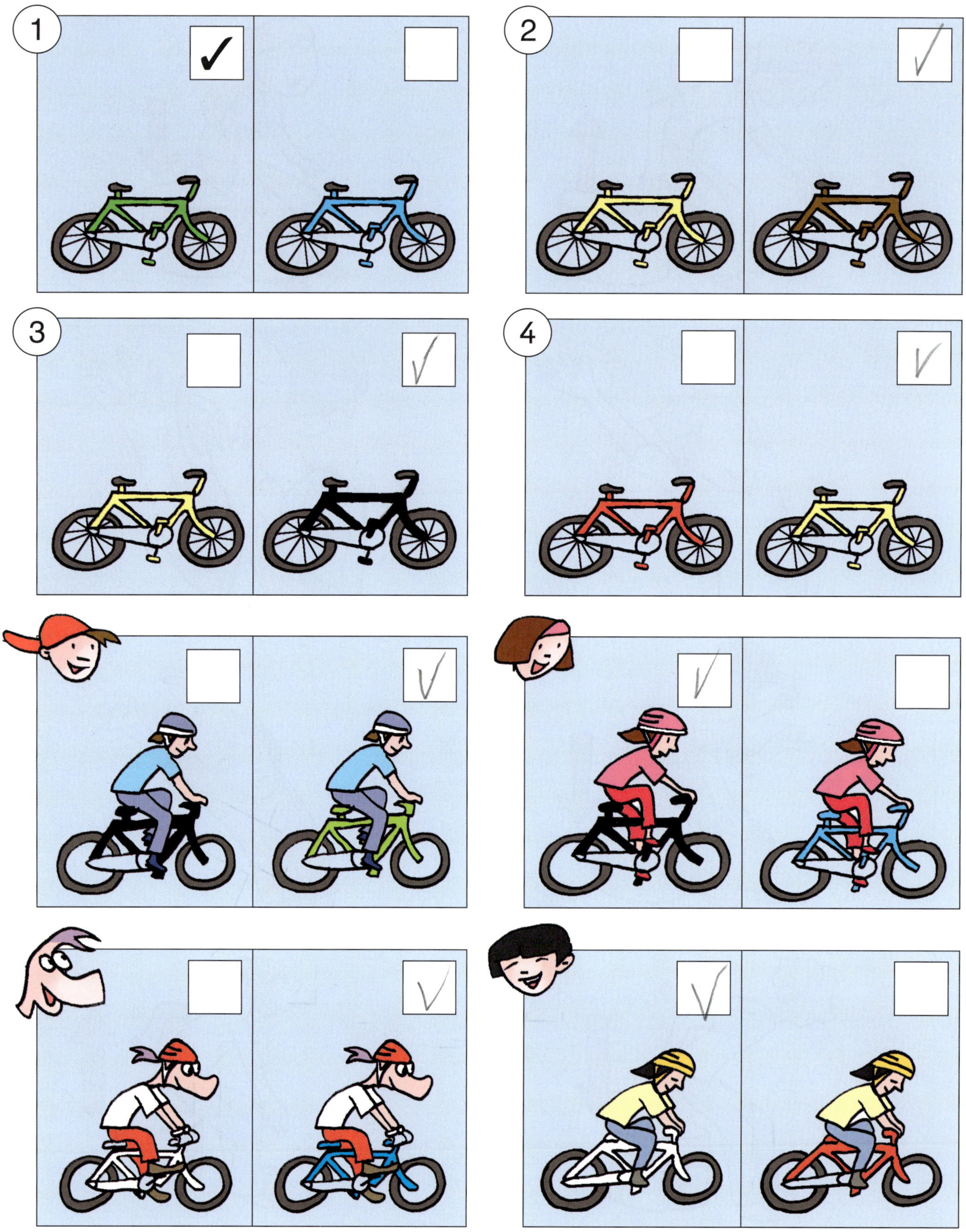

3 Listen and tick (CD 1/2).

4

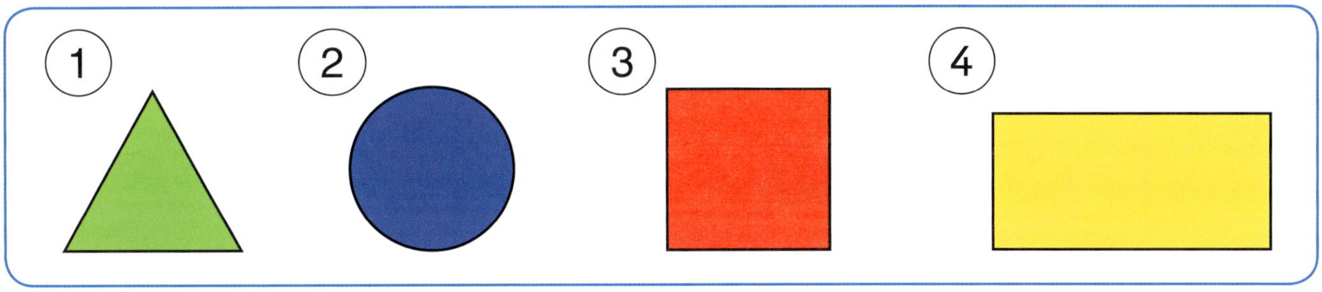

4 Look and colour.

School

1

2

❶ Look and remember. Speak. ❷ Colour and speak.

3

3 Listen and tick (CD 1/3).

4

4 Listen and colour (CD 1/4).

5 

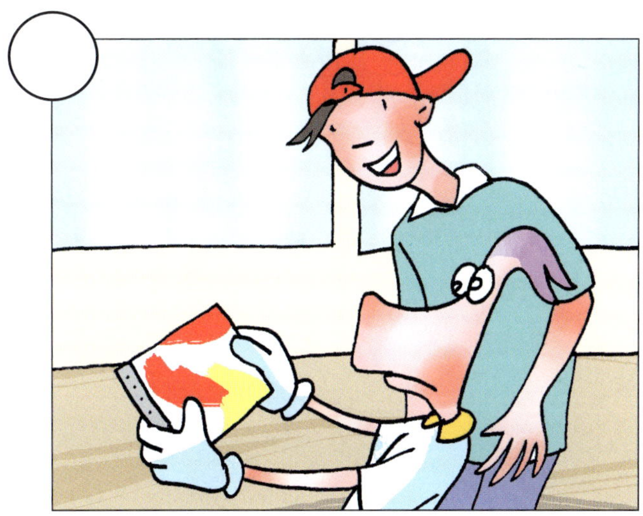

1 

5 Listen and fill in the numbers (CD 1/5).

Unit 3

Fruit

1

❶ Listen and fill in the numbers (CD 1/6).

2

❷ Listen and draw (CD 1/7).

3

3 Listen and tick (CD 1/8).

4

4 Listen and fill in the numbers (CD 1/9).

Unit 4 Pets

1 

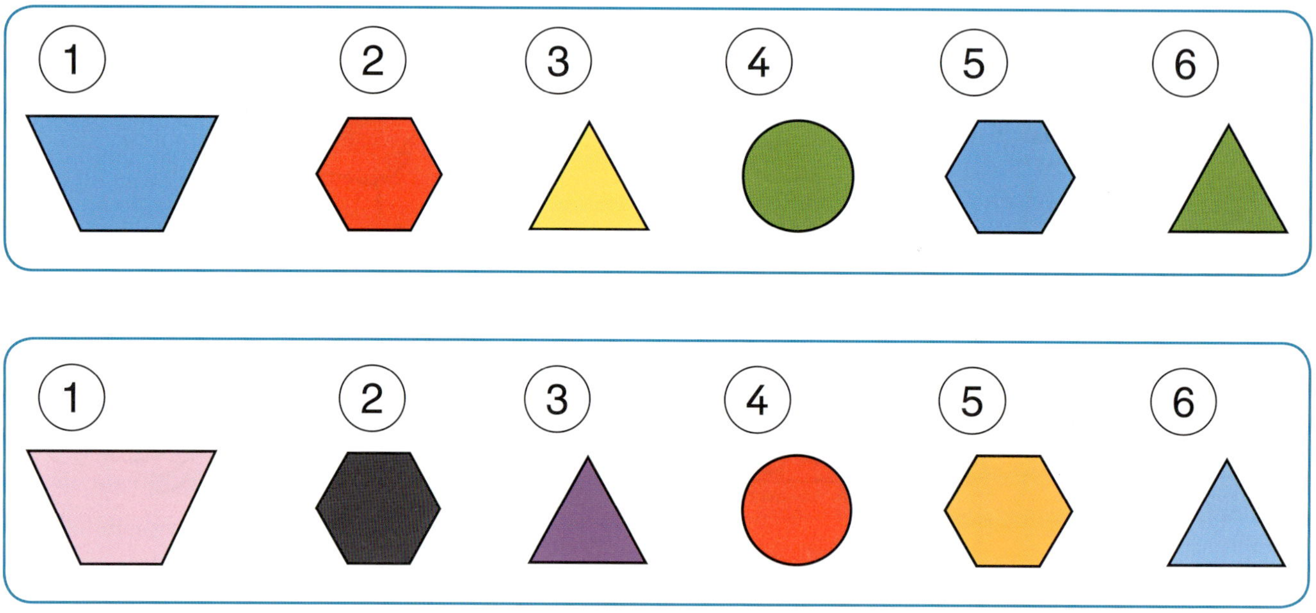

1 Look and fill in the numbers.

2

1

2

3

4

5

6

7

8

❷ Listen and tick (CD 1/10).

3

3 Listen and fill in the numbers (CD 1/11).

4

4 Listen and draw (CD 1/12).

Unit
5 Toys

1 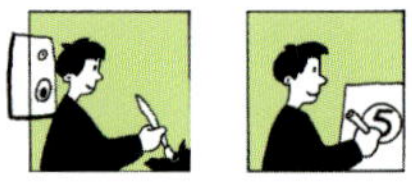

1 Listen and colour (CD 1/13). Find, fill in the numbers and colour.

2 

1

2

❷ Listen and circle (CD 1/14).

3

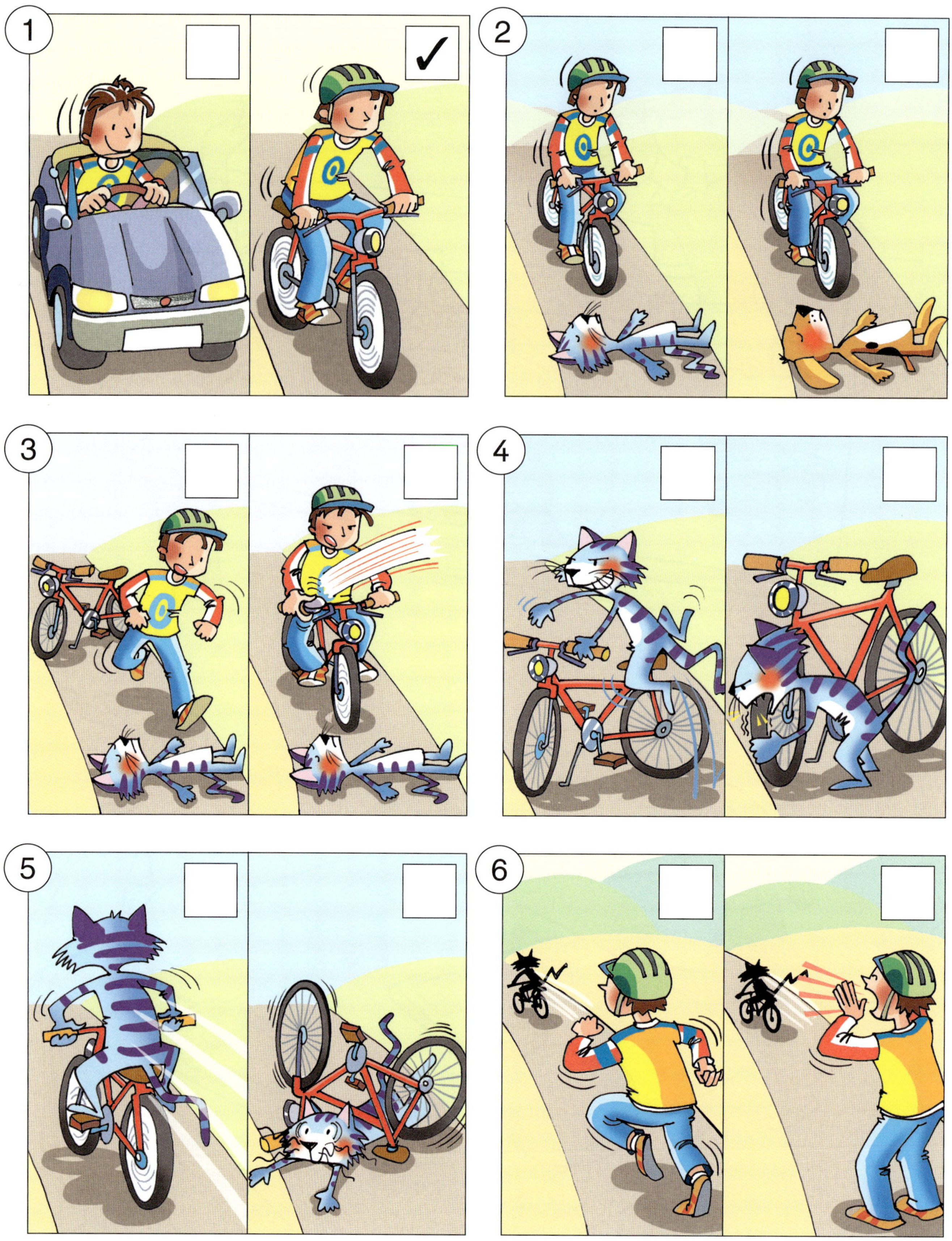

3 Listen and tick (CD 1/15).

4

1

2

5

❹ Listen and circle (CD 1/16). ❺ Draw, colour and speak.

Unit 6

Winter

1

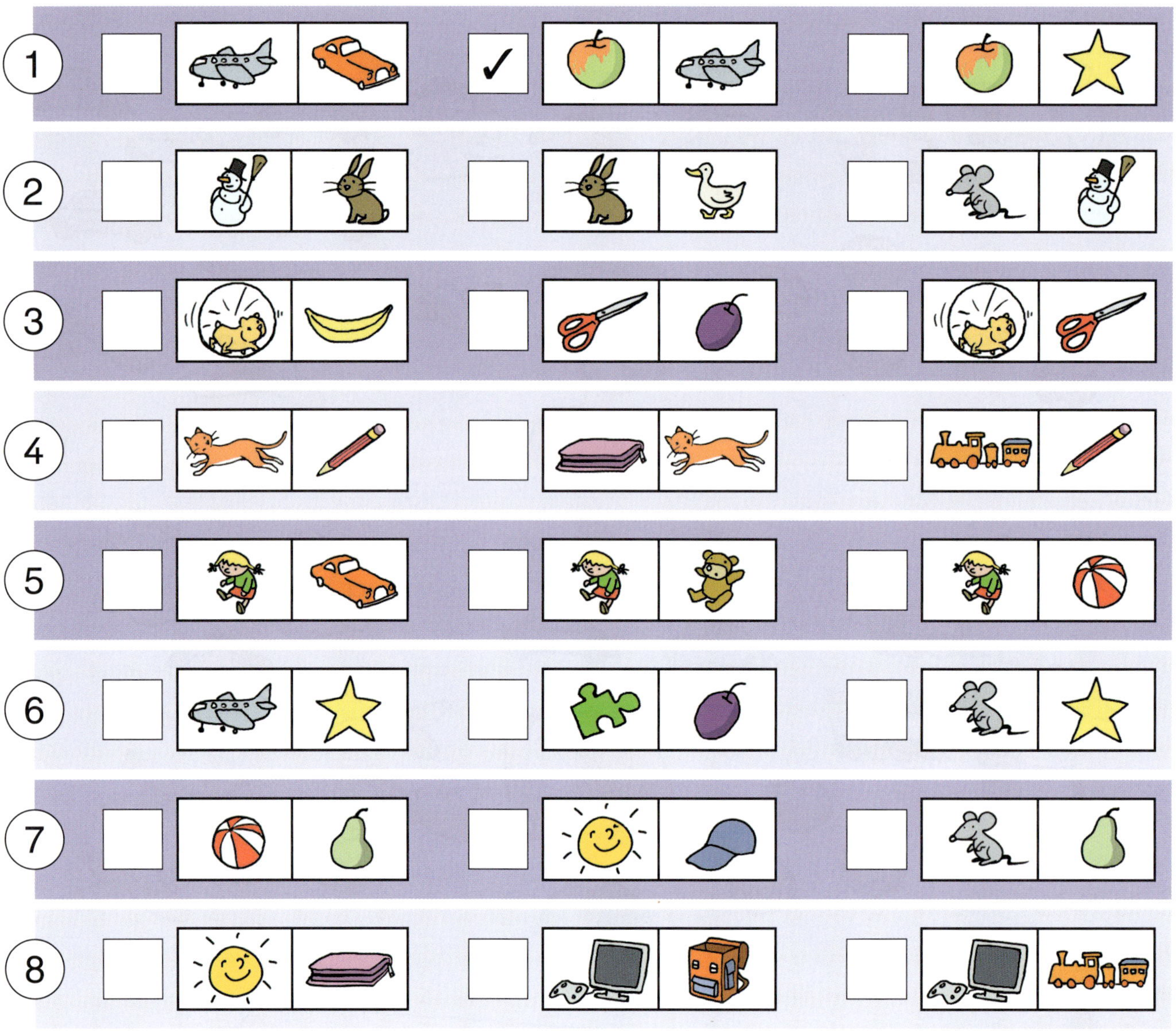

2

❶ Listen and tick (CD 1/17). Speak. ❷ Draw and speak.

3

3 Listen and fill in the numbers (CD 1/18).

Party

1 

1 Listen and colour (CD 1/19).

2 

❷ Listen and fill in the numbers (CD 1/20).

3

2 + 7 = 9	1 + 6 =	6 + 3 =
8 + 1 =	5 + 2 =	4 + 3 =
3 + 6 =	4 + 1 =	3 + 5 =
7 + 2 =	4 + 2 =	4 + 5 =

4

❸ Do the sums. Speak. ❹ Listen and complete the picture (CD 1/21).

Health

1 

❶ Listen and fill in the numbers (CD 1/22).

2 

1
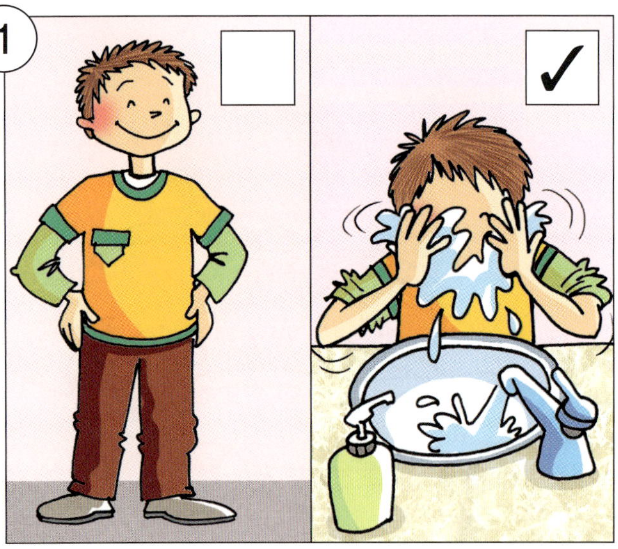

2

3

4

5

6

2 Listen and tick (CD 1/23).

3 

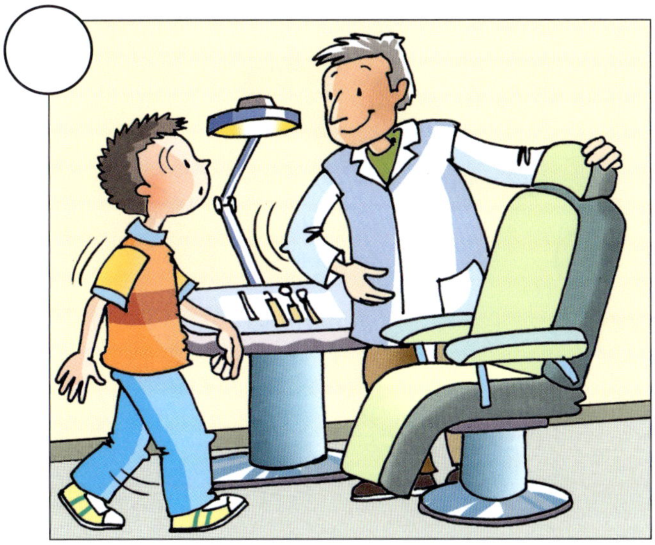

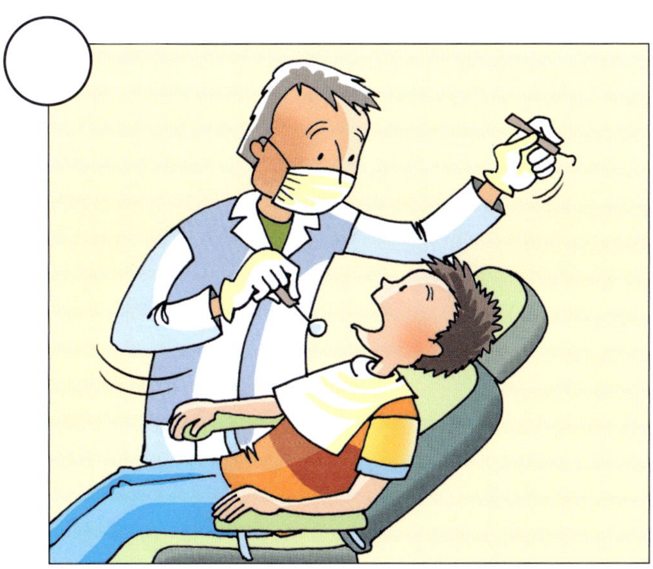

3 Listen and fill in the numbers (CD 1/24).

4 

4 Think and draw. Speak.

Weather

Unit 9

1

❶ Draw to complete the pictures. Speak.

2

❷ Listen and colour (CD 1/25). Count and fill in the numbers.

3

3 Listen and tick (CD 1/26).

Unit 10

Food

1

1

1 Listen and fill in the numbers (CD 1/27).

❷ Listen and match (CD 1/28).

3 

3 Colour and speak.

4 

❹ Find the odd one out.

Animals

1 

1 Colour and speak.

2

1

2

3

4

❷ Listen and tick (CD 1/29).

3

❸ Listen and fill in the numbers (CD 1/30).